NATIONAL GEOGRAPHIC LEARNING

OUR WORLD

My Body, Your Body

by Cynthia Makishi

NATIONAL
GEOGRAPHIC
LEARNING

I have a body.

I have a body, too.

3

My eyes are brown.
Are your eyes brown, too?

4

No, they aren't.
My eyes are red!

My mouth is small.
Is your mouth small, too?

No, it isn't.
My mouth is big!

My hair is long.
Is your hair long, too?

No, it isn't.
My hair is short!

I like my body!

I like my body, too!

Facts About Bodies

Read the names for the parts.

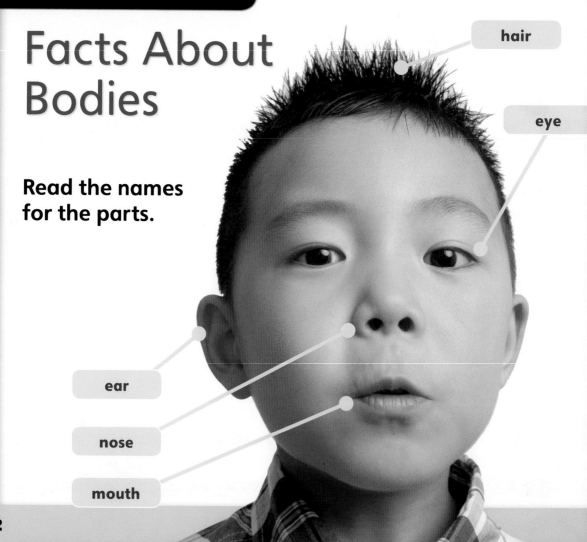

hair

eye

ear

nose

mouth

ear

fur

eye

**Some are the same.
Some are not!**

snout

mouth

Fun with Bodies

What can each part of the body do? Match.

listen

| mouth | nose | eyes | ears |

smell

sing

see

Write the word for each part.

ear   eye   hair   mouth   nose

hair

Glossary

name

part